Then and Now

Having Fun

Vicki Yates

Heinemann
LIBRARY

Chicago, Illinois

© 2008 Heinemann Library
a division of Reed Elsevier Inc.
Chicago, Illinois

Customer Service 888-454-2279
Visit our website at www.heinemannraintree.com

Designed by Victoria Bevan and Joanna Hinton-Malivoire
Photo research by Ruth Smith and Q2A Solutions
Printed and bound in China by South China Printing Co. Ltd.

12 11 10 09 08
10 9 8 7 6 5 4 3 2 1

ISBN-10: 1-4034-9832-6 (hc) 1-4034-9840-7 (pb)

The Library of Congress has cataloged the first edition of this book as follows:

Yates, Vicki.
  Having fun / Vicki Yates.
    p. cm. -- (Then and now)
  Includes bibliographical references and index.
  ISBN-13: 978-1-4034-9832-8 (hc)
  ISBN-13: 978-1-4034-9840-3 (pb)
 1. Leisure--Juvenile literature. 2. Leisure--History--Juvenile literature. 3. Recreation--Juvenile literature. 4. Recreation--History--Juvenile literature. 5. Amusements--Juvenile literature. 6. Amusements--History--Juvenile literature. I. Title.
  GV182.9.Y38 2008
  790.1--dc22
                                        2007014730

Acknowledgements
The publishers would like to thank the following for permission to reproduce photographs: Alamy pp. **9** (Martin Harvey), **11** (Steve Skjold), **19** (Mike Watson Images), **22** (Arthur Steel; Comstock Images p. **23**; Corbis pp. **10** (Owen Franken), **18** (Hulton-Deutsch Collection); Flickr p. **13** (Jimmy McDonald); Getty Images p. **20** (Paul Martin/General Photographic Agency); Irish Press Archives p. **5** (Thérèse Sheehy-Devine); Istockphoto pp. **7**, **23**; Library of Congress pp. **8**, **12**; Photolibrary.com pp. **6** (Index Stock Imagery), **15** (Franck Dunouau/Photononstop), **21** (Dynamic Graphics); Science & Society p. **16** (NMPFT Daily Herald Archive), **17** (Ian Hooton/Science Photo Library); Shutterstock pp. **4** (Alex Melnick), **23**; Staffordshire County Records Office pp. **14**, **24**.

Cover photograph of boy with hula hoop reproduced with permission of Getty Images (Photodisc Blue) and photo of boy playing football reproduced with permission of Corbis (Jim Cummins).
Back cover photograph reproduced with permission of Irish Press Archives/Thérèse Sheehy-Devine.

Every effort has been made to contact copyright holders of any material reproduced in this book. Any omissions will be rectified in subsequent printings if notice is given to the publishers.

Contents

Having Fun 4

Games and Toys 6

Entertainment. 14

Let's Compare 20

What Is It?. 22

Picture Glossary. 23

Index 24

Having Fun

Today people like to have fun.

Long ago people liked to have fun, too.

Games and Toys

Long ago people played board games.

Today people can play computer games.

Long ago people moved toys
by hand.

Today people can move toys by remote control.

Long ago toys were made of wood or metal.

Today toys can be made of plastic.

Long ago children played outside.

Today children play outside, too.

Entertainment

Long ago people watched plays.

Today people can watch
movies, too.

Long ago people listened to the radio.

Today people can watch television, too.

Long ago people listened to records.

Today people can listen to CDs.

Let's Compare

Long ago people had fun in
many ways.

Today people still have fun in
many ways.

What Is It?

Long ago children played with this toy.
Do you know what it is?

Answer on p. 24

Picture Glossary

CD a small plastic disc that has music on it

play a story told at the theater

record a black plastic disc that has music on it

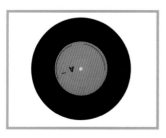

remote control a machine used to control something from a distance

Index

CD, 19

game, 6, 7

movie, 15

play, 14

radio, 16

record, 18

television, 17

toy, 8, 9, 10, 11

Answer to question on p. 22: It is a hoop-and-stick game. Children rolled the hoop with the stick.

Note to Parents and Teachers

Before reading: Tell children about the games you used to play when you were at school. If possible, show them games such as Hopscotch, Jacks, and Marbles. Ask them to name their favorite games.

After reading: Use the question on page 21 to prompt a discussion about the differences between toys from the past and toys today. Ask children to point out how they are the same and how they are different.

You can support children's nonfiction literacy skills by helping them use the table of contents, headings, picture glossary, and index.